Table of Contents

Introduction

From the time my kids learned to speak, the moment they would say, "I can't" I would interrupt them with, "What, do you come from Cantville?" I would then explain how all things are possible. I have repeated that phrase to them their whole life and although they are now grown, they still expect to hear those words whenever they say, "I can't." That one silly word "Cantville," was the genesis for this book.

Cantville tells the story of two towns separated only by a mountain and the attitudes their people hold. Do not let the format of a "picture book" deceive you or give a preconceived idea. Within every page are seeds of self-improvement insight to make this book much more than it first appears. The story is a unique vehicle to deliver positive messages in a non-confrontational, simple to read format.

All ages can enjoy this book on every level. Small children under age five can experience the fable of two towns and the beautiful illustrations. Children ages six to 12 can appreciate the underlying lessons. Teenagers can examine their prevailing attitudes and try a more positive outlook. And just as important—adults tired of the barrage of daily negativity can be reminded that there is a more productive and enjoyable way of thinking.

I purposely did not write a central character so you can experience and relate to the messages in the book on an individual level—without seeing it through the eyes of anyone else. As the reader you can attach the traits of each town to yourself and the people in your life. You can allow the words to evoke thoughts, ideas, and feelings which may be dormant or suppressed due to a busy lifestyle. I ask you to be open, be positive, and enjoy *Cantville* on whatever level you choose. I also recommend that over time you reread repeatedly until you can get through the book cover to cover, without it stirring up new thoughts or ideas. Don't be so certain you gained all you could from the first reading.

The intention of this book is to encourage you to think for yourself and reaffirm that there is always a choice—regardless of circumstances. The purpose was not to lecture or *tell* you anything, but instead to make available positive ideas and thoughts in a simple and relatable format. The book never says, "Hey, you're bad and you need to change!" But rather, "Hey, you're fine as you are, but here are some thoughts you might find interesting."

You may have read other books on positive thinking or motivation, but because of the presentation the information may have been forgotten minutes after reading, and left you uninspired. This is why I wrote in the form of a fable. It allows you to take time to think about your own situation without losing your place in the story. It is also the easiest for any age to comprehend, absorb, retain and recall.

Regardless of your age, current attitude, or knowledge, you will get the most from *Cantville* if you keep an open-mind to recognize and consider the messages. I suggest you do not read it as a *know-it-all* or *cynic,* as you will be wasting your time. No book is for everyone and this one needs to be read with an optimistic attitude. If you do this and intend to get something positive out of the story, you will—it's really that simple! And yes, you can and should read this to young children… over and over!

It is so important to instill positivity in children as early as infants. They won't understand at first, but in time they will pick up on the feelings and it will form a habit where being positive is the norm. As you'll read in *Cantville,* we should be mindful about saying, "no" and, "can't" so often to small children. Hearing these words over and over in the developmental years may stunt a child's curiosity and creativity not only as children, but well into adulthood.

Along with reading, writing, and math, we should teach children the benefits of having an optimistic attitude, personal confidence, self-motivation, and the power of positive thinking. A child who is confident and motivated will be happier, healthier, and more successful in every aspect of life.

I hope *Cantville* can be one small step in a person's journey to become a positive, happy adult—even if you are already an adult! If nothing else, I hope this book reminds you of the wonderful gift each day brings. If we simply keep our focus on what we have, and not what we are lacking, we realize there is never a good reason to be negative.

Sit back, relax, and enjoy the inspiring tale of *Cantville*!

So we shall let the reader answer this question for himself:
Who is the happier man,
he who has braved the storm of life and lived
or he who has stayed securely on shore and merely existed?

-Hunter S. Thompson

Chapter 1
Two sides of one mountain

"We are the same, except for our differences"

Far away on a beautiful secluded land of mountains and thick green forests, there lived two towns. Each town was completely isolated from the other by a huge mountain called Mount Decision. On one side of the mountain was the town of Cantville, and on the other, the town of Wecando. Neither town knew the other existed, but both had access to the same resources of fresh drinking water, warm weather, rich soil to grow fruits and vegetables, and lakes filled with a bounty of fish. Both towns were exactly the same, except for one thing… attitude.

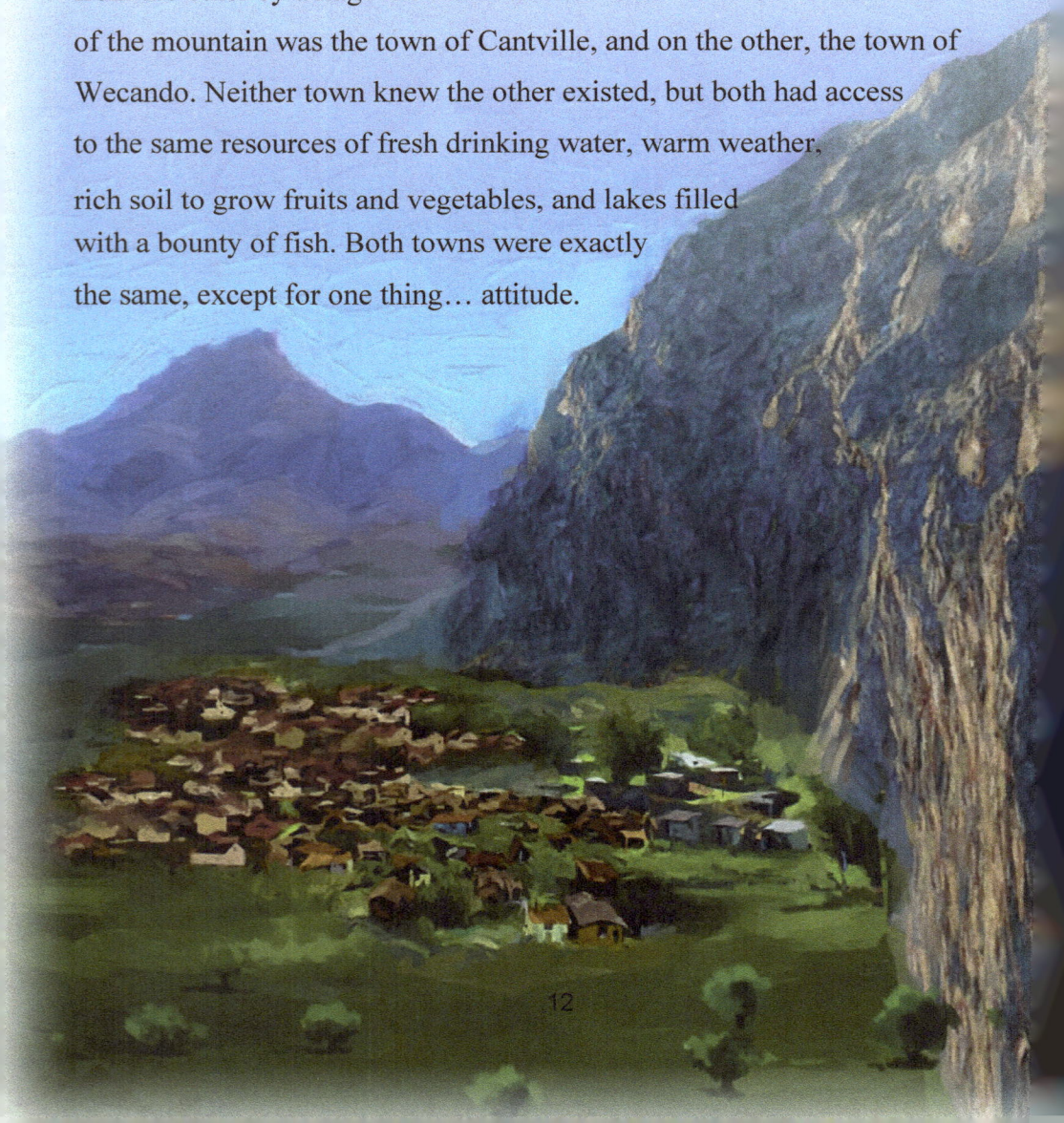

But it wasn't always that way. Early in their history, both
towns were wondrous places where people lived in happiness and
fulfillment. The warm, sun-filled mornings made it a joy to wake up
and explore the vast opportunities, where every person had the
freedom to do and be anything they wanted. They worked hard,
enjoyed life with friends and family, and lived productive
and content lives. Their independence from the rest
of the world inspired each person to take
responsibility and succeed on their own.

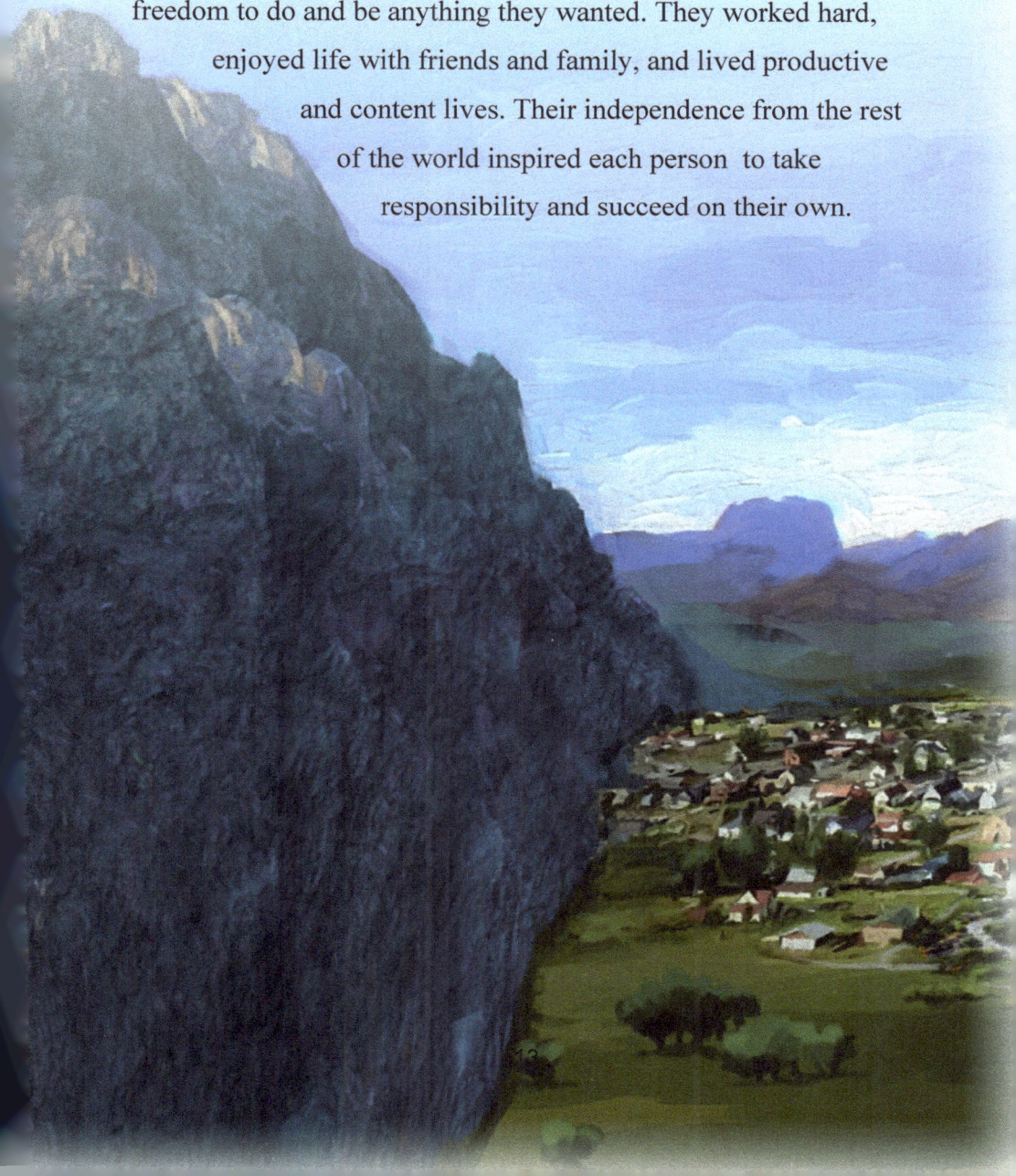

The people of Wecando, known as Wecandoers, embraced their independence through easy times as well as hard. They discovered long ago that it was during the difficult and challenging times when their confidence and self worth grew the most.

On the other side, life in Cantville changed the moment they encountered their first major hardship. During this time the people lost confidence and allowed fear and worry to alter their way of life. This shift in thinking took place over one winter without anyone realizing it was happening. Throughout this devastating time, the Cantville people, who called themselves Cantvillians, focused their decisions on, "quick fixes" without considering the lasting consequences. These choices over one winter changed the course of Cantville's future for years to come. The winter when everything changed was the winter of the great storm known as the Deep Winter Freeze.

It came without warning and was the harshest storm ever recorded as it settled over Cantville and Wecando. No one prepared themselves for such devastation as the storm lasted nonstop for seven grueling weeks. Each day was colder than the one before as daily icy temperatures dropped below zero. The snowfall was constant as it piled higher with every hour.

It was at this point where life in the two towns veered in opposite directions. This change of path was not *caused* by the Deep Winter Freeze, as both towns experienced the same great storm. This change was due to each town's *reaction* to the storm, and their ensuing attitude.

The Wecandoers worked individually and as a team to survive the storm with minimal long-term harm. Regardless of how difficult this time was or how punishing the storm became, they stayed positive, supported each other, and never felt sorry for themselves. They kept a "We-Can-Do" attitude and an unwavering faith in their ability to do whatever was needed. In fact, the people of Wecando came out of the storm stronger, smarter, and better equipped for future challenges.

During this same time the Cantvillians became cold, hungry, scared, and desperate for help. They tried to stay optimistic and work together but the endless snow and bone chilling temperatures made it seem as if the storm would never end.

Everywhere they turned there was another reminder of their tough situation. After a few days, the feelings of fear and desperation overwhelmed them. These emotions became stronger than their belief in themselves—which led to their longstanding trust and faith in their own abilities to be forgotten. Their change in attitude from positive to negative altered the way they saw themselves, and how they were perceived by others.

Once they lost their confidence and acted out of fear, they became easy targets to allow others to take advantage… and take advantage they did!

While most of Cantville was suffering through the Deep Winter Freeze, not everyone in town had it so rough. There was a small group of people who owned all the stores that sold firewood, blankets, medicine, and food. These store owners chose to only trade with each other during the storm, which allowed them to stay warm and comfortable. Sadly, as the storm continued and the town's people became more worried, the store owners saw this as an opportunity to enhance their wealth and power. They held a secret meeting and decided they would only distribute the needed items if the residents of Cantville voted to elect them as their "General Counsel of Leaders," or just, "Leaders" as they became known. When presented to the people, they resisted at first, but after a few weeks of being cold and not knowing how much longer it would last, they accepted their help and allowed the Leaders to take control of their town.

Chapter 2
Cantville and the Leaders

"Small decisions could lead to big problems"

The Leaders helped as promised, but while doing so they taught the Cantvillian adults not to have trust in their own ability and to depend only on the Leaders to make their decisions. They also instructed the children from a very early age that only the Leaders could do everything for them—and without their help, they did not have the talent nor skill for challenging tasks. Whenever Cantvillians would try something new, the Leaders would tell them, "No, you're doing it wrong" or, "Stop, you're not ready" or, "You will hurt yourself, let us do it for you." So, generation after generation came to believe that they could never do great things for themselves and should wait for someone else to do it for them.

This thinking trained the people to have negative attitudes, which affected how much they believed in their own talents and potential. Due to their low self-esteem, they would never try hard to accomplish things on their own. They had forgotten that this was not the natural attitude with which they were born—they were born to be positive, productive, and loving. The Leaders taught and reinforced this negative attitude over many years until Cantvillians completely lost their personal sense of worth and confidence to decide for themselves.

Unknowingly, the Leaders also kept them unaware that all the years of negativity could be turned around at any moment in time, as quickly as snapping a finger, just by choosing to change their attitude from negative to positive and intending to have a happier life.

Because of their bad attitude, Cantville homes and buildings began to fall apart. If something broke, the people would say, "I can't fix that" and they waited for the Leaders to fix it for them. The people of Cantville were often hungry because most did not have the motivation to plant food, hunt, catch fish, or do anything to make their lives happier. If asked to do something, they would respond, "I can't do that, I was never taught."

They took no personal accountability for their own well-being. They allowed and relied on the Leaders to take care of all their needs. This way of thinking also permitted them to blame the Leaders for not doing enough. They knew if they did not take responsibility, they could then place fault on others instead of on themselves.

The people of Cantville should have had the most fantastic town. Cantvillians were good and honest people and clearly had many hidden talents which had never been tested or developed. Even with all the negativity, their people's true qualities could not be hidden.

There was Max Emum who had the biggest muscles anyone had ever seen. Surely, he was strong enough to carry the heavy materials needed to build sturdy homes.

However, if asked, Max would say, "I can't" and, "I won't" and he would have a million excuses why he would not do something.

Samantha Smartypants was one of the most mentally gifted people in the whole wide world. It would have been easy for her to think up ideas on how to make Cantville great. However, when asked to do so, Samantha would reply, "I can't" and,

"I won't" and she would have a million reasons why she could not help.

Then there was Tori Fick who excelled at fishing, but after catching one or two, she would say, "I can't catch anymore" and, "I'm not good at fishing." If she had confidence, she would catch a hundred fish a day and no one in Cantville would ever be hungry.

Everyone knew Luca Median as the funniest person in Cantville. He was so entertaining that people would gather from all over town just to hear him tell stories so funny that everyone would roll on the ground laughing. But after a few minutes he would stop and go home. When friends would tell him that he should put on a show and charge money, he would say, "I can't do that, no one would pay to see me. I won't be able to make a living being funny. I can't and I won't."

21

Finally, let's not forget Willy Growmore who may have been the best farmer ever to farm. All of his fruits and vegetables grew to incredible sizes. He once grew a pumpkin the size of a baby elephant! Instead of being proud and farming more, he saw his large peaches, pears, carrots and that giant pumpkin as a negative, because of their abnormal size. He convinced himself that he was a terrible farmer because he could not grow food in the *regular* sizes. He would mumble to himself all day, "I can't be a good farmer, I will never be good at farming. No one will like my giant fruits and vegetables."

In fact, every single person in Cantville had a special skill or talent which he or she was wasting. They all had interests in things, and for a split second they might allow themselves to dream about actually doing them—but then their negative thoughts and attitude would creep back, and they would again think, "I can't."

They hardly ever tried anything new or challenging. When they did gather-up the courage to do so, they would quit the minute they had the smallest setback because they did not believe in themselves.

Any day of the year, if anyone had listened in on Cantville, they would have heard over and over, 100,000 times a day, "I can't, I won't, I can't, I won't, I can't, I can't, I can't, I won't." The people actually made a song with just those words and sang it day after day, drumming those negative thoughts into their heads.

No one in Cantville realized that the little voice in their head telling them "no," "I won't," and especially, "I can't," was not their own. It was the voice of their scared, overprotective, controlling Leaders who repeatedly put unhelpful and negative thoughts into their heads from birth.

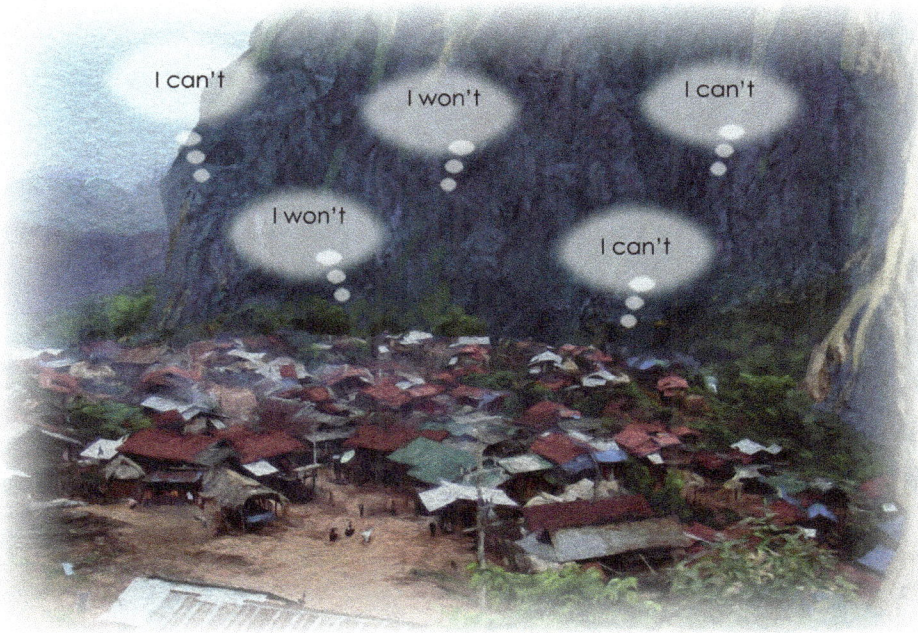

For the citizens of Cantville, saying "I can't" was a perfect excuse for not trying new things. "Why won't you?" they might be asked, to which they would reply,"Because I can't." Cantvillians believed no one could argue with, "I can't." So they went about their daily routines without ever thinking about why they did the things they did.

Cantvillians did not understand how powerful those negative thoughts were—and by thinking them over and over, they had actually created and made real the very things they did not want to happen.

During the Deep Winter Freeze, Cantvillians felt as if they had no power and no other choice. They were not aware that there is always a choice and in most cases, power is not taken, but rather it is given away.

The people of Cantville would one day learn that the easy choice is not always the best—and out of the thousands of decisions made each week, one never knows which will be life-changing, so consider them all wisely.

Chapter 3
New Neighbors

"Be bold and mighty forces will come to your aid"
-Basil King

On the other side of Mount Decision, Wecando also had their version of leaders called "Partners," but they only guided the community and never forced their views on to other people. The town held elections each year, giving every interested person a fair chance to have their voice heard.

During the Deep Winter Freeze, the Partners suspended most of their positions and worked along-side the citizens. Once the great storm ended, life in Wecando went back to normal. They considered the Deep Winter Freeze as one of life's misfortunes to deal with—and when it was over, they put it behind them. They did not let one destructive event ruin their way of life—instead they were grateful for what they still had, and for the the opportunity to learn and move forward. Wecandoers returned to appreciating the pleasures of their land and their people. Everyone in the town had a job to perform and a purpose in life. They helped their neighbors when help was required, and other times let people do for themselves.

Wecandoers were taught from an early age to try new things and experience life. They were raised to believe that the only failure was in not trying. If they attempted something and fell short, it was okay. If they tried something a hundred times, getting an undesired result each time, it was still okay—as long as they kept trying and learning. It was only okay to quit when they no longer loved what they were doing—but never because it was too hard. Most Wecandoers knew that *failure* was really just the opinion of other people, and they should not react, or judge their efforts based on what others think.

The people of Wecando loved new experiences. They continually challenged themselves to try different things and invent amazing products. It was quite different in Cantville. If a Cantvillian had never seen something, they believed it to be impossible—while Wecandoers always imagined themselves doing the impossible! In Wecando, impossible meant, "I'm-Possible!"

One thing Wecandoers always dreamed possible was to discover what was on the other side of Mount Decision. It was so big that it completely cut-off each town from the other. No one in either town knew what existed over the mountain.

Cantville looked at Mount Decision and thought of it as a barrier. If anyone wanted to see what was beyond the mountain, they would have to wait for someone to come from the other side. People in Cantville had such fear of the unknown that most would not even think about what existed over the huge peaks of Mount Decision. Of those who did, some assumed the mountain never ended, while others thought it was the edge of the world—but most were too scared to even think about what horrors could be waiting for them… and they had no desire to find out!

On the other hand, Wecando looked at Mount Decision and had such wonder about what could be on the other side. For years they had fantasized and made up stories about what could be over that gigantic, mysterious mountain. They speculated about finding another town of friendly people, or magnificent new animals and trees, or even something so amazing they could not even imagine!

One day during a town picnic, they all started talking about Mount Decision and trading stories of the fantastic mysteries that could be on the unknown side. One after another, the people of Wecando got excited about exploring and doing what no one in history had ever done before… getting to the other side of the mountain!

As the bell in the clock tower hit noon and rang out, the people of Wecando declared, "This is no longer a dream, we are going to do it! We will figure out a way to get to the other side of Mount Decision!" In that one moment, all the years of thinking of Mount Decision as an obstruction to seeing the other side had vanished. When they changed their thinking and made it a priority, they actually changed their reality. They realized that the mountain had never been the real barrier—it was the way they *thought* about the mountain that held them back from doing the impossible.

They broke off into groups and got busy discussing different plans to get past the mountain—and on that sunny spring afternoon, they believed they had figured it out!

One group thought about going around or over it—but they calculated that due to the enormous size of Mount Decision, it might take years and be extremely dangerous. Another group thought about going right through it—but that might take longer and be more dangerous. Then a little Wecando girl said, "Why don't we just move it?" Instead of telling her to be quiet and let the grown-ups think, they listened. Then they thought about it. Then they considered it. Then they all cheered, "We will move the mountain!"

They decided they would dig holes to put lifts under the mountain, then raise it and slide it out to the sea. However once they started digging one little boy meekly suggested, "Why don't we just continue digging and make a tunnel under the mountain?" Before reacting and telling the boy that they knew better, the workers stopped and thought about it. After thinking and discussing for a while, they stopped digging and put the project on hold. They then went back to the drawing board to figure out if they should stay on course, or if digging a tunnel was a better plan. Within a few days they emerged to proclaim that the boy's idea was not only possible… but it *was* the better way!

Wecandoers never got stuck in one way of thinking. If a better idea came along, regardless of where it came from, they would take time to consider it, and change direction if needed. They never rushed into important decisions—their motto was, "It is better to suspend, than amend."

The next day they continued to dig, but got stuck for days when they were stopped by a solid rock that seemed as big as the moon. Once they got around the rock, they were flooded with tons of rushing water, which came at them with the force of a mighty tidal wave. The crashing, unforgiving water carried them tumbling out of the tunnel, and down the street.

After the water cleared, they went back under the mountain digging and running into other surprising setbacks. They were beset by bats, muddled in mudslides and daunted by darkness. One after the other, day after day—it seemed as if the obstacles would never end!

Before starting, they knew this would not be an easy challenge—but getting past Mount Decision was a thousand times harder than anyone had ever expected or planned. However, all through the endless trouble they never lost faith. They were passionate about their goal to see what was on the other side, and nothing would stop them.

Then, on the four-hundred and eighth day of digging, they broke through and saw daylight on the other side. They all stopped and stared. Their long backbreaking work had finally come to an end—but strangely at this point they became a little scared. "What is on the other side?" they asked. "What if we made a mistake and something bad is there?" they cried. "Maybe we should have left well enough alone!" they feared.

"What if, what if, what if!!!"

The Mayor of Wecando, Kara Boutyou, then shouted, "We are from Wecando! We will bravely deal with whatever is on the other side and will not let fear of the unknown stop us! All of our 'what ifs' are just negative thoughts. They are not real unless we give them the power to be real. We cannot doubt ourselves at this point. In our hearts we know we are doing this for the good of Wecando!"

Michelle Teachthem, the school Principal then spoke up, "Even the most confident person may have moments of doubt—but it's what a person does at the point of fear and doubt that defines them. A person can either think negatively and allow their thoughts to stop them—or they could be positive and continue to do great things. In either case, the situation is exactly the same, it's just the thinking that is different. So I choose to do great things!"

With that, everyone took a deep breath, regained their confidence, and went forward to emerge out of the tunnel, right into the middle of Cantville.

Since Wecandoers look just like Cantvillians, they blended in without being noticed. The Wecando people walked around town and observed Cantville, which appeared to have access to the very same resources as Wecando. There was clean water, plenty of good soil for farming, nice weather, beautiful forests, and lots of capable people. However, Cantville didn't look anything similar to Wecando. It was run-down and dirty, and seemed as if it was lost in time. They noticed none of the modern advances of Wecando. The Wecandoers continued to explore for hours only to become more puzzled and captivated as to why everything was so different when the two locations appeared to be exactly the same.

The Wecandoers, now feeling safe in their new surroundings, decided to find out everything they could about this fascinating place. They walked up and down the streets asking questions and speaking to random Cantvillians. After an hour of meeting people, the only thing they had learned was the town's name, and all the things the people couldn't do.

Wecando business owner Joe Vial then suggested, "We should not assume we can learn from the opinions of a just few people. If we want to find out about this town, we must gather as many citizens as possible from different backgrounds, for a town meeting."

Chapter 4
The Meeting

"Listen when opportunity speaks"

It wasn't the slight bit difficult to get everyone together, since the people of Cantville were accustomed to being told what to do. Word spread swiftly, and without asking "why," people gathered in the park and gave their attention to the new visitors. One by one, taking turns, Wecandoers asked the citizens of Cantville questions, starting with, "Why is your town not up to date?" Cantvillian Al Armist replied, "Because we can't fix or build things very well." Another asked, "Why are the store shelves so empty?" A store owner answered, "We can't find enough people who want to work." One daring Wecandoer then asked, "Why doesn't anyone here seem happy and content?" This led the men and women of Cantville to look at each other to find an answer, but instead ended up just shrugging their shoulders as if to say, "we can't answer that, we don't know."

After a few hours of questioning and learning about Cantville, they found that the average Cantvillian didn't really care about his or her situation. Given that it was the Leaders who controlled and distributed all of the goods and services, the Cantville people saw no reason to put forth effort and try new things, knowing they would not reap the full benefits of their risk and labor.

They had become so used to things and accepted their life as it was, with no thought of it changing. Not a single Cantvillian knew there were other ways of living, or of the personal satisfaction one gets from taking full responsibility for themselves and their loved ones.

The Deep Winter Freeze was long before any of these people were born, and no one was ever taught about life in Cantville prior to the great storm. Some had heard tales, but assumed it was folklore and could never have been real.

By this time, Wecando had enough information to understand life in Cantville. It was now their turn to speak about Wecando—and they felt confident the people would be receptive.

They were excited to tell about their many new inventions that made life easier and more productive. They joyfully spoke of their stores with shelves fully stocked with delicious foods. Wecando finished by explaining in detail the teamwork that not only helped them achieve unimaginable goals such as tunneling under a mountain, but also helped them manage their day to day lives, so that every Wecandoer had the freedom and opportunity to prosper and live life as each saw fit.

The people of Cantville stared in amazement and listened as if they were being told a fantastic science fiction story. Not a single Cantvillian asked a question.

Wecando went on to explain what they had noticed during their short trip in Cantville. They told them that right there in Cantville, they already had the resources to grow nutritious food, live in comfortable modern homes, have beautiful parks and schools, and anything else they wanted.

This finally got the Cantvillian's attention and they started to ask questions. Alex Adaisical spoke up and asked, "That all sounds nice, will the people of Wecando build those houses, parks, and schools for us?" Anna Notherthing asked, "Can Wecando grow delicious food for us... and will you come back and cook it for us too?" Then all at once, every Cantvillian shouted out questions, all asking Wecando to do things for them.

Wecando's Mayor Kara Boutyou interrupted saying , "Whoa now, why do you want us to do everything for you?" Which she was quickly sorry she asked, because the whole town of Cantville responded with the force of thunder, "WE CAN'T!" They shouted so hard and loud that the force of their breath knocked down the people of Wecando.

When the Wecandoers got up and steadied themselves, Mayor Kara Boutyou stated, "We only offer to teach you to do for yourselves, not to do it for you." That was all Cantville needed to hear. The disappointed crowd slowly broke up and walked away with their heads down. They would not allow their minds to consider that they could learn something new and take responsibility for themselves. Cantvillians grumbled, "What a waste of time, we can't do any of what they said" and, "It's not fair they have so much while we have so little," and many other negative comments.

Cantvillians had no faith in themselves or their neighbors. Not one would believe that their future could differ from their past experiences. They may have heard all the words Wecando said, but because they listened with a negative mind, they did not hear the opportunities they offered.

Chapter 5
Realizations

"It was there the whole time, you were just looking with your eyes closed"

At this point the people of Wecando went back through the tunnel knowing they had tried their best to help their new neighbors. Before they left, they spoke to every citizen of Cantville telling them that they would leave the tunnel open. They expressed their happiness to assist anyone who changed their mind and wanted to learn to do for themselves.

Cantvillian Terry Bulthoughts then spoke up and asked, "For how long is your offer good?" Wecando Banker Nick Elsndimes replied, "Actual change takes just a moment in time. It happens as soon as you decide in your mind, and in your heart. But it may take days, months, or even years to *truly* be prepared to make that decision—therefore the offer is an open invitation with no time limit."

Throughout the walk back, Wecandoers discussed how it is very hard to change another person's mind, and they shouldn't force it. After all, they didn't think life in Cantville was *wrong,* they were only offering suggestions. Wecandoers accepted that people like to live all different ways—that's what it meant to be independent and inclusive. No one should judge another just because they choose to live differently.

During the trip, people from both towns got to know one another and became friends. Although their apparent core beliefs on how to live were quite opposite, they were able to put that aside and learn about the other person on a deeper, personal level. They focused on what they had in common, not their differences.

Wecando understood they could only *offer* their knowledge and allow each Cantvillian to make up his or her mind as to what was best for their own personal situation. Whether or not they accepted their advice did not affect their friendship. They liked the Cantvillians for who they were on the inside—not where or how they lived.

The following years saw a few dozen Cantvillians travel through the tunnel to Wecando where they discovered how to develop their personal talents. Some stayed in Wecando to live, while others returned to Cantville to help their neighbors. These Cantvillians soon noticed that while some individuals welcomed new ideas, others were perfectly happy with the old Cantville way of life. To them, this was perfectly fine as they now appreciated and respected each person as an individual.

Even those people who did not choose to change still made a choice… they just chose to stay the same. Cantville Librarian, Paige Turner remembered a quote she had read in the Wecando library which said it best, "Life is made of many choices—those we make, and those we choose not to make."

As time passed, countless Cantvillians were open-minded enough to learn from Wecando—and their lives changed for the better. It was now clear there was more to life than what the Leaders had taught them to believe.

They started to take an active role in their life by asking questions—which led to better, more informed decisions. By taking risks and saying, "yes" to fearful challenges, they discovered new personal interests and talents. The Cantvillians became aware and confident in their abilities, and embraced them with a positive attitude, and with the intent to succeed.

Most importantly, they found that helping others was more valuable than being helped. They no longer waited for a helping hand, but instead offered one.

With this great attitude change, Cantvillians learned it was just as easy to be positive and happy as it was being negative and sad—but being positive was more fun! When other Cantvillians saw their friends happy and productive, they also decided to give this new way of thinking a try. One by one, Cantville as a whole was on its way to becoming a positive town.

The transformation to positive thinking brought many changes to Cantville. Every achievement big and small brought new excitement and enthusiasm to do more. The people took pride in everything they did while being filled with the confidence to realize their dreams—even if it meant risking what others may call, "failure." They learned to simply be grateful for the gift of each new day—and to stop *wanting* happiness and just *be* happy.

Soon, spacious homes and tall buildings were under construction, streets and parks were cleaned, store shelves were filled with new products and food, and new friends were being made every day.

Chapter 6
The New Goal

"Every goal reached is another stepping stone"

A town meeting took place in the Cantville park, which was now restored to spectacular beauty with bright green grass and multi-colored flowers. During this meeting they learned the true meaning of the name, "Mount Decision." Samantha Smartypants gave a speech announcing a new yearly holiday called, "Mount Decision Day."

She explained to Cantville citizens, "A person's life is determined mainly by the decisions they make or don't make. Each and every choice we make, regardless of how big or small, changes our future in some way. Enough of these decisions will create the direction of our life—and determine how happy, successful, and complete our life becomes. This mountain is our testament that making good decisions and having good intentions leads to a good life."

As a reminder to everyone going through the tunnel, they hung a sign with the words, "Decisions and Intentions" onto the side of Mount Decision.

In that same meeting, citizens of Cantville chose to take back their personal control. Their first order of business was a vote to change the town's name to, "Canville." Just saying the town name made people happy. They were amazed at the difference one little letter could make! It reminded them that even a tiny change could have a huge effect.

It was not a coincidence that the day the town's name changed was the same day the General Counsel of Leaders lost their power over the people.

Canville soon held new elections and voted for optimistic leaders who were supportive and positive. The General Counsel of Leaders surprisingly backed the change, as even they now realized that personal responsibility was best for everyone, including themselves.

Former Leader Milo Viewofyou said, "We now see that letting people do things for themselves and allowing them to fail or succeed on their own merit, does so much more for a person's personal growth than trying to protect them from failure by doing tasks for them. The term, 'I was just trying to help' is not always so helpful. The Leaders may have had all the answers, but we see now—they weren't all the *right* answers. It is best for our society as a whole, to honestly listen and consider every view, without prejudgment or prejudice."

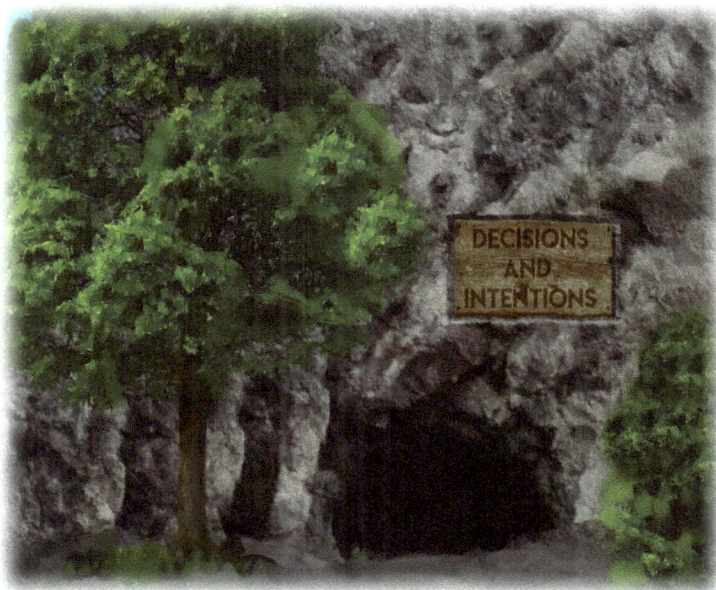

The next week they threw a big party to celebrate the town's name change and invited everyone from Wecando. The people of Canville—now called Canvillians, served scrumptious food and drinks which they made on their own. Willy Growmore donated a truck-load of his famous "Biggie" fruits and veggies, while Tori Fick had the world's best fish fry!

Canville children had full control over decorations for the party. They gave the park a festive look using ideas learned from their new arts and craft classes. They were all so proud of their creations! It was a feeling of accomplishment that none of them had ever known before— which warmed their hearts with wonderful feelings of happiness and joy.

As the full moon gave light to the crowd of happy faces, the new Mayor of Canville, Alice Well, gave a heartfelt acceptance speech, "We've come a long way in a short amount of time, and we are just getting started! But regardless of what we accomplish, in the end, our value to this world will not be determined by what we took for ourselves, but rather what we gave *of* ourselves. Physical items will weather with time. Wealth passed on, but not earned, will cause more trouble than good. Our *true* value to this world, will be the wisdom, attention, and love which we gave freely, without wanting anything in return. This is what will live forever inside those close to us... and eternal when they pass it on to others. Enjoy life and all it has to offer, but don't lose yourself in the process.

We have much to be thankful for in Canville. As your Mayor, I promise to stand alongside you when you need help—behind you when you need a push—and in front of you when you need guidance."

She then capped off the evening by announcing, "Now that we've seen what is on the other side of the mountain, we want to see what is on the other side of the stars! We are setting a goal to put a Canville flag on a distant planet beyond the stars within the next ten years!" Everyone cheered for the goal with excitement, as they now truly believed that with a positive, confident attitude and a clear intention, there were no limits—not even the stars!

Chapter 7
Sometimes, the teacher learns the most

"Happiness is not found, it is within us. Love is not in us, it is us"

It was not only the citizens of Canville who benefited from their contact with Wecando. It turned out that many Wecandoers learned helpful things as well. By getting to know the Cantvillians, they learned how to be more open about asking for help. They also learned better ways to farm and catch fish. And maybe most important, they witnessed first-hand a different way to think about life and how to appreciate quiet moments alone without thinking about their next responsibility. These ideas and skills were just as important to the well-being of Wecando as the things they taught to Cantville. They all learned that everyone had something positive to offer—even if it didn't seem that way at first.

Both towns understood that in every situation there was a lesson to learn. Sometimes it might be hard to find, but if one looks, it would be there waiting for them, and it would be just for them. Everyone may get something different out of a situation, and that's perfectly okay. The key is to keep an open mind, and if need be, step back from the issue and look at it from the outside without your personal opinions. Many times this will allow a person to understand the circumstances with an open and clear mind.

In Canville, the most wonderful thing happened. As new babies were born, their parents raised them with positive values and motivations. The story of the Wecando people and the day the tunnel appeared became a popular Canville tale which parents told their children every night before bed. Just from hearing the story over and over, and being raised in optimistic surroundings, the children grew into adulthood to be positive, hardworking, and happy. As did their children, and their children's children, and their children's children's children, and so on!

A lot went into the transformation of Canville, and it took many years... but it all started with a simple change in attitude!

Still today both communities continue to live in harmony. The tunnel of Mount Decision is constantly busy with people crossing both ways—because learning, deciding, and changing should never stop. The two towns don't agree on everything, but that's a good thing! If everyone always agrees with each other, then no one ever learns anything new. What's important is that they respect each other's differences and judge no person based on those differences.

Now, what about that goal of going beyond the stars? Well, if you ever gaze up into the night sky and see a bright light shooting across the stars, you can be sure a Canvillian is up there waving down to you!

Therefore, if anyone should ever tell you that you can't do something, you look them straight in the eyes and tell them with confidence, "I don't come from Cantville, I can achieve anything I set my mind to do!" And, when you find someone in doubt of them self saying, "I can't," help them by asking, "What, do you come from Cantville?" Then tell them this story.

The End...
Your beginning!

After thoughts...

This story is a personal one. As a small boy and teenager I was raised and lived in "Cantville," where nothing much was expected from me and most things were viewed through a negative lens. In my twenties, after years of searching and researching, I found my way to Wecando—and that is where I chose to stay! I am living proof that it is possible and never too late for a person to change their entire outlook and attitude.

All the views in this book are from personal thoughts I truly believe and try to put into action every day. It wasn't until I spoke to publishing and writing professionals that I realized I would have to rely on those beliefs to complete this book.

I found most people in this industry (as I've found in most industries) seem to live in Cantville. The conversations usually started with, "no" and everything after had to do with comparing my book with what is, "standard."

I was told this book was too long as a picture book and too short as a chapter book. I was told I had to have central characters with which people could identify. I was told it did not adhere to the typical age standards and target a specific reading level—and worst of all, I was told, "I recognize this writing as a passion project for you and so my opinion is you should do whatever you see fit with it in terms of form and format." This to me meant, "No one will read this, so it doesn't matter what you do." I used all of those comments as additional motivation to work harder and make this book the best I could.

From my experience I found that the publishing business makes *business* decisions. They play it safe and have no interest in anything different. But I've seen the unusual or the, "outsider" win too many times. I refuse to change this book just because it doesn't firmly fit into a standard category. I put my time and money betting that the reader knows best and he or she will enjoy this tale in the current length and format.

Books have changed my life, so it was important for me to produce something of value that honestly cares about the reader, rather than a safe, uninspired "cookie-cutter" book devoid of risk.

Could all those professionals be right? Maybe... but then again, maybe not! I will never know if I just accept their judgment as fact and quit because of it. By blindly accepting someone's opinion is stating that you believe that person is never wrong. I don't know anyone who is never wrong, including experts, so I choose to believe in myself and see where it takes me. In this sense I still think as a child does. Children often answer, "no" with, "why?" I continue to do this because if you ask, "why" enough times you'll find there are other (and usually) better answers besides, "no." The next time your mind tells you, "no" keep asking yourself, "why" until you come up with a better solution—or until you find that, "no" is really the best answer.

Could working jointly with a professional publisher have made this book better? Heck yeah! But they were either not accessible or did not believe in the book, so it was not an option. That left me with two choices... quit or complete it to the best of my ability.

Whether this book fails or succeeds commercially, I did it my way—and I did it with the *Wecando* attitude. Did I make all the right decisions? Probably not, but I took my time, did my best, and worked honestly… and that is all I can ask of myself. The worst outcome is that I publish a book I loved creating and believe in 100%. I also learned a few new skills along the way! If this book gives hope or brightens just one person's day—or gives someone an hour reprieve to reflect and forget about their daily stresses, it will be well worth the effort.

Now that you've finished the book, you have a few choices. You can walk away thinking it was a nice little story or you can deem it a worthless waste of time. Or, if you choose, you can be inspired to implement a more positive attitude into your daily life—and not just during the happy times when it's easy, but also throughout the challenging times. Even if you already have an optimistic outlook, you can always bring it to a higher level and be more positive. You may find that having a bad day is a thing of the past if you make a conscience effort to control your thoughts. It may not happen overnight so don't become discouraged—continue taking small steps in the right direction and good things will happen.

It is all up to you, it is your choice—and that is the core message of the book. Whether you choose to do or choose not to do, it IS a choice. Make it wisely and own it.

Remember, there are no excuses. Even if you find an excuse—don't believe it! Excuses are almost always negative and transfers power away from you and gives it to the excuse. You can decide to be positive or negative in any situation and as a general rule in life. This one decision will influence and guide much of how things turn out in your life. Always be aware of your decisions and intentions.

I don't know you, but I believe you have the ability to do or be whatever it is you want. How do I know? Because we are each born as a clean slate with unlimited potential. Some are born with more challenges, but our successes are not to be compared with others, but to our full potential.

Much of how we are today, good and bad, is due to outside influences such as family, friends, teachers, the media and entertainment world and more. Think about your beliefs and where they originated. Are they really yours—or were they instilled by others and you are just living out someone else's thoughts? Strip away everything negative that has been imparted on you by others—actions, habits, prejudices, fears, dislikes, and most importantly thoughts—and you will be left with the real you, and that is a great place to start.

Glossary

—The definitions in this glossary differ from what might be found in a standard dictionary.

The descriptions, thoughts and ideas are the opinions and beliefs of the author and are not to be intended as fact. They are provided as provoking comments to stimulate thought, discussion, and reflection. To that end, each definition includes questions or statements to prompt the reader to think about their meanings on a higher personal level. Take a moment to reflect on each word and how it relates to your life.

Attitude—The manner in which a person thinks. You can have a positive attitude—which is happy and excited, or a negative attitude—which is sad, angry or gloomy. You can also have a neutral attitude where you have no strong feeling about anything. Your attitude towards a person, place or event will determine how you react, and it's outcome. Your attitude comes from your experiences and your thoughts. When you have a feeling towards something, stop and think about why you feel that way, and from where those feelings come. Then decide if you truly feel that way or if it's just an automatic reaction from a past experience.

—You can change your attitude just by altering your thinking. If you decide you want to be positive, you just need to think and believe positive thoughts—and your body and mind will accept it and follow! Give it a try the next time you have to do something you don't want. Change your attitude towards it, and the whole situation will change with you! You can use this towards your job, school, siblings, parents, friends and everything else. Always be aware of your attitude and be free to adjust it to make your life more enjoyable.

Accomplish—To complete a task or achieve a goal. To accomplish is a very proud and happy occasion since it is usually the result of hard work. Accomplishing a goal or task is not always as powerful as the process. Many times you learn and get more satisfaction from the process, and the accomplishment is just the "cherry on top." While working towards your goal it might be hard, unpleasant, or tiring, but if you remain strong and positive you will have a success. With that said, if the accomplishment becomes more important than the process, you might cheat, cut corners, or not give your best effort just to finish. It is only an "accomplishment" if you honestly do your best.
—Is there something you need to accomplish? If so—get started!

Assume—To assume is when you believe something without having facts—and are making judgments entirely from your imagination. Assuming is often not a good quality and typically leads to trouble and unneeded stress. If you have some facts or a long history with a person or situation, then you might have educated guesses, which are fine and often correct. Assumptions (to assume) are many times brought on by fear, lack of confidence, or wanting too much control.
—When was the last time assumed? How did it work out for you?

Barrier—This can be something solid such as a wall which stops you from entering. It could also be a person who obstructs your development. Or it could be a mental limitation such as attitude, fear or worry. Anything that gets in your way of progress is a barrier—but as we learned from *Cantville*, barriers are only permanent if you allow them.
—Can you name a few barriers in your life now? Can you get around them by changing your thinking?

Benefit—Something good or helping. You can be a benefit to other people or to a cause. Things such as a car or pet, or places such as stores, libraries, or hospitals could be a benefit. Some items or people could be good (a benefit) for some and not for others—it all depends on the circumstances.
—What do you enjoy more; when you are a benefit to someone, or when you are benefiting from someone else? Why is that?

Blame—When you hold someone (including yourself) or something responsible for a negative action. It is a harmful term used in anger or sadness to reduce personal responsibility. If the facts are clear and it is the responsibility of another, then it's just that, facts not, "blame." It is never a good idea to blame someone or something else if you have a part in the problem. It is better for your soul to take responsibility and forgive yourself. Blame leads to resentment—resentment leads to hostility—and soon the person you're blaming is off enjoying a happy life while you're stuck in bitterness.
—Were there times when you blamed someone because it was easier than accepting responsibility?

Confidence—To truly have trust and belief in yourself (personal confidence) or in another person, institution, or situation. When you have personal confidence, you stand tall and do not doubt. Other people can sense real confidence and are drawn to it like a moth to light. To be confident is not to be a bully, "know-it-all" or "loudmouth," as these are commonly people with low confidence. When confident, you know what you are capable of and you don't seek or need the approval of others. Having a positive attitude will build your confidence!
—Is there any area in your life where you should be more confident than you are?

Content—When you are satisfied and do not yearn for more than you have. Content people are happy because they focus on what they have, not what they don't have. Being content does not mean settling for whatever you have, but rather to be happy and grateful for what you have. A content person can still have goals to have more—which differs from just wanting or wishing for more. If you want more, then go out and get it and be happy that you have the opportunity to work for what you want.
—Do you focus on what you don't have more than what you do? Can you change that thinking to be more grateful so you can be more content? And by the way—when you reach contentment, more things come your way naturally. It's the universal law of attraction.

Define—To explain or describe. In *Cantville,* the story defines the qualities of the communities. People are defined by many attributes—including their looks, intelligence, humor, compassion and much more. How do you define yourself?

—Do others think of you different from the way you define yourself? If so, think about how you can better express your qualities?

Develop—To grow or expand—to bring out possibilities. Talents or ideas are developed by practice and learning. If left alone and ignored they will stay the same, or worse—deteriorate. There are no short cuts or cheating when it comes to developing your skills. They will not develop into something higher without you personally working on them.

—Is there a talent or personality trait you want to develop? What is holding you back?

Doubt—To hesitate and to be uncertain or to question a belief. It's okay to have doubts if you're lacking facts or if something seems odd—that's being cautious. Someone you should never doubt is… yourself. Doubting yourself means your confidence is low or non-existent—as doubt is the opposite of confidence. It is hard to succeed in any task if you don't believe in yourself.

—What doubts do you have about yourself? Why do you have them and where do they originate? Do you have some doubts to protect yourself from risking and failing?

Excuses—When you attempt to remove fault from yourself or someone you are protecting (see "Blame.") In most cases you know the truth but can't admit to the facts. In other cases you don't want to believe the truth so you lie to yourself by making excuses. In either case it's not helpful to anyone. It is always best to accept the truth and place the responsibility to whoever deserves it… even if it is you.

—Think of times when you've made excuses? Can you admit to yourself that the excuse was not real and you were just protecting yourself? Now can you forgive yourself and if needed, make it right and be honest with whoever deserves it.

Failure — Some people define "failure" as attempting something and not completing it, or doing it incorrectly. As learned in *Cantville*, failure only comes in not trying or not doing your best. A person should not be afraid to fail since that thought alone may literally lead to failure. Failing while learning is a key to success. Thomas Edison "failed" over 1,000 times and when asked about it he replied "I did not fail 1,000 times, the light bulb was an invention with 1,000 steps." Babe Ruth struck out over 1,300 times and is still known as arguably the greatest baseball player of all time. The world is filled with successes who had to fail many times. As we learned in *Cantville*, "failure" is really just an opinion or a state of mind. It is only real if you allow it to be.

—Has the fear of failure ever held you back from trying something? Can you make a list of these times and if still important, try to accomplish a few? If you attempt and fail, what's the worst that could happen?

Faith—TV character Archie Bunker once said, "Faith is something that you believe in that nobody in their right mind would believe." Faith is trusting and believing with all your heart without needing proof. Faith is usually connected to religion but it applies to so much more.

—What or who do you have faith? Who might have faith in you?

Fear—Fear is a basic emotion that you feel during times of danger, pain, fright or any other situation that is out of the norm and unknown. Fear feels exactly the same whether the fearful situation is real or perceived. Sometimes fear is good as it keeps you safe (fear of getting hit with a car keeps you from running into traffic.) Fear is often a product of past circumstances (Getting bit by a dog as a child still produces a fear of dogs as an adult) but is just as often a basic part of your personal emotions. Fear is personal—some people may be afraid of the dark or heights, while others are not. It is the same as when you find a joke funny and others don't. If fear is holding you back from reaching productive or worthy goals—you should try to overcome it through research and assistance. But if you honestly try and that feeling won't change, don't be ashamed—it's just a part of who you are. Maybe that fear is there for a reason we can't understand.

—Is there something you are fearful of that you want to change? If you try and can't get past the fear, can you give love and support to yourself as you would if it were someone else?

Free-will—Free-will is the ability to choose what is best for you regardless of what others think and without being held back by outside factors. It is the choice to think and be as you want—to be free. "Choosing" to give up your free-will, is still having free-will.

—Are there times now when you are giving up your free-will? Is it by choice, by necessity (which is still a choice) or is it forced?

Grateful—When you truly appreciate and are thankful with no thought of, "what's in it for me." To have gratitude is humbling and is the gateway for joy and happiness. While holding feelings of gratitude, it is impossible to be angry or sad.

— Set aside negative thoughts and worries and think about all you have to be grateful. Your health, friends, family or just the fact you are alive and full of possibilities.

Harmony—This word is often associated with music—but in general terms it is when all parts work together smoothly and perfectly. To be in harmony with another person leads to a stress-free, mutually pleasing relationship. To be in harmony with your world including family, friends, work, school, and most important, yourself, is a most worthy goal to attain.

—Are there parts of your personal world that are not in harmony? Can you repair those parts? Can you let go of parts that are no longer aligned with your harmonious world?

Impossible—In general, this describes things that can't be. But we learned in *Cantville* that, "impossible" is just a frame of mind. Anything is possible! Things we now take for granted such as cars, airplanes, televisions, computers and more were once thought impossible just a few hundred years ago. I bet in your lifetime you've seen or will see things thought of as impossible just a few years prior. Believing in the "impossible" and not listening to the, "no" voices, is the secret behind most great successes. Napoleon Hill said, "What the mind can conceive and believe, the mind can achieve." It would do you good to remember that quote and repeat it to yourself everyday.

—Is there something you want in your life that you think is impossible? Why is it impossible? Keep asking "why?" until maybe you see it really isn't so impossible. Now, make believe anything is possible—no restrictions. Are the things you made up really impossible? What can you do to make it happen?

Independent—An independent person is free to be who they choose. They are not influenced by the opinions of others and do not take part in group mentality thinking. They take care of themselves and like it that way. As a friend or love interest, they spend time with you because they want to, not out of need. An independent person appears confident and strong. Many people believe independence is one of the most admired qualities in a person.

—Are you more comfortable being independent or depending on others? Why is that? Where does your independence or dependency originate?

Intend—When you intend, you honestly expect to do or have something happen. Intentions differ from wants, wishes, hopes or dreams where you passively wait for your goal to magically appear. Intentions are powerful thoughts where your mind is actively engaged and focused. You must intend, believe that intention, then put yourself in the position to receive the results. As long as you truly believe in what you intend, it will happen.

—Have you intended to do something and never followed through to completion? Do you see how they were really wants, wishes, hopes or dreams and not true intentions? Make an intention now and believe it as if it is fact. When going to the mall, I always intend to get a good parking spot… and I always do! Start small and work your way up to larger intentions!

Mistake—A mistake is a non-intentional error. Obviously everyone makes mistakes, but not everyone learns from their mistakes. What you learn from the mistake is usually more meaningful than the error. If your mistake hurt or affected someone else, then it's your place to take responsibility and make it right. Take full responsibility for your mistakes, learn from them, and don't repeat them (or at least not too many times!) and you'll be fine. Avoid making excuses for your mistakes—as that would be… a mistake!

—Have you apologized for, or corrected all of your past mistakes? If not, do it now. Have you forgiven those who made honest mistakes against you? If not, do that too.

Motivation—To be motivated is more than "wanting." It is the internal drive that inspires you go after and follow-through on whatever you choose. A person is motivated by many emotions; love, hate, anger, happiness—but it simply comes down to either wanting to gain something, or not wanting to lose something.

—What motivates you more—the desire to gain or win, or the fear of loss? There is no right or wrong answer, but you should know your core motivation so you can act accordingly.

Negative—Very simply, negative is the opposite of positive. If you only see the bad and refuse to look for good, then you are being negative. But, just because you don't agree with a person or situation, or if you don't like something, this does not make you negative—it makes you independent. There is a positive or a, "silver lining" in most situations—do yourself a favor and always look for the positive. Negativity is like a disease that infects other parts of your life and health. Being negative is a choice—so choose differently if you want happiness. It may not change the circumstances, but it will change the way it affects you.

—Are you feeling negative towards someone or something? Can you find a positive? Can you feel grateful for the positive more than feeling bad about the negative?

Obstacle—Anything that gets in your way is an obstacle. It could be physical or it could be a thought. Similar to an, "obstacle course" the things in your way are not the end—they just force you to discover a different way to move forward or to overcome. If you look at obstacles as challenges, they will become opportunities, not problems. Let no obstacle stop you—let it make you stronger.

—Do you have any mental or physical obstacles in your life? Can you find your way around them and turn them into opportunities?

Opinion— "A belief," "A judgment," "A personal view." You'll notice the word, "fact" is not found in the definition. If a teacher scores your test at 75%—that's a fact. If she says "you can do better"—that's an educated opinion from an expert and should be considered. If she tells you that your shirt is ugly—that's an opinion which you decide if it's correct or not. Don't believe opinions before checking for yourself. You can and should have opinions on things, but it's up to you whether you want to share them or keep them to yourself.

—Are you doing or behaving in any way due to of the opinion of others? Are you forcing your opinions on anyone else?

Passionate—An emotion that overwhelms with the totality of your feelings and belief. To have passion is one of the greatest joys in life. You can have passion for a person, a job, a cause or anything else. Passion is so personal it should not be explained and just needs to be found on your own. Identify your passion, embrace it and all else will fall into place.

—Are you passionate about anything? If not, why?

Positive—Good and optimistic. As we read in *Cantville*, being a positive person starts and ends with your state of mind. Having a positive attitude attracts positive things. People react better to positive people which in effect will bring happier days. Sometimes bad or negative things are going to happen regardless, but staying positive can shorten that negativity so it doesn't ruin the rest of your day… or life. Everyone benefits by being more positive.

—Make a goal to start each morning with a positive outlook and keep it all day long. Think only positive thoughts and if a negative one should slip in, yell, "Stop" in your mind and rethink the same thought with a positive twist. In *Cantville* we saw that you can change your attitude in seconds just by changing your intentions. Intend to be positive!

Prejudgment—To enter a situation with your mind made up before you've heard all the facts. When you prejudge you believe you know more than anyone else. It is okay to pre-analyze a situation and to picture the outcome—but keep an open mind so that you don't miss opportunities.

—The last time you prejudged someone or something… were you right or did you miss something because your focus was on your judgment instead of the truth? How would you feel being prejudged and not have the opportunity to present your ideas to open minds?

Prejudice—To hold prejudice is to form opinions on other races, religions, social statuses or appearances (and maybe other things) based on preconceived views not based on reality or on an individual person. To dislike anyone individually based on personal experience or facts is not being prejudiced regardless of who they are. To dislike and judge people, either individually or as a group, solely due to what they look like or where they come from, and to treat them badly or unfairly because of those thoughts—that is prejudice.

—Are you prejudice against any group of people? If so, think about why. Was it taught to you as a child? Where do those underlying feeling come? Do you really feel that way?

Productive—To move forward and get things done. The best tool for productivity is making a list. A list will keep you on track and confirm your productivity. Being productive is not always moving and working— sometimes a little rest to recharge your batteries is the most productive thing you can do! Being productive is how we get things done.

—Where do you have issues being productive? What holds you back in those areas?

Reinforce—To make something stronger. The best time to reinforce is not when it's breaking, as it might be too late and you are, "fixing." One of the most important things to reinforce are relationships. Not when they are falling apart, but when they are strong so they will never fall apart. Don't take strong people or relationships for granted. Reinforce them by giving encouragement, support and extra love on a regular basis so it never needs fixing.

—Find a few relationships to reinforce and do it with passion!

Resources—Many may think of resources as physical things you have such as money, a car or friends and family. But your true resources are your mind, willpower, confidence and the ability to love and care. These are the core resources needed for any task and you already possess them!
—Have you let the lack of, "resources" stop you? Can you now tap into your internal resources and accomplish what you didn't in the past?

Responsibility—To take care of what is yours or what you are accountable. No excuses, no blame—you own it, good or bad. Regardless of where you are in life, don't blame history, accidents or other people. If you are personally wronged, it is your responsibility to find help and/or justice. You are responsible for yourself and your minor children and anyone or anything else you choose. Just keep in mind—when you take responsibility for someone else, you are allowing them not to be responsible for themselves. Do you remember what happened in *Cantville* when the Leaders took over all responsibilities?
—Are you too responsible or not enough? Are you trying to save everyone in your world from sinking while you slowly drown? Be responsible but also encourage others to do the same.

Routine—Doing things in an order on a regular basis. A routine could be just as good as bad. Routines are very structured and at times very needed. But sometimes being in a routine is the same as being in a, "rut." It becomes boring, lifeless and saps enthusiasm. Some people only get great ideas out of an unstructured environment and are very uncomfortable in structured settings. At the same time, other people need a routine where they feel comfort in knowing what they should be doing at every moment.
—Are you stuck in a routine when you don't want to be? Do you need to make a routine to be more productive?

Trust—Confident that things are as they appear and no harm is evident. Every day you trust without thinking about it. You trust the food you eat is fresh, the medicine you take is safe, the drivers on the road are alert, and so on. There's hardly anything more important than trust, and once it is lost, it is very hard to get back. Your best friend is probably the person you trust the most. Be trustworthy and trust those that are worthy. Liars and cheaters think nothing of trust—so think nothing of liars and cheaters. —Can you think of a few people you trust and whether you appreciate them enough? Are there people who trust you and are you worthy of that trust?

Value—The worth of something either in monetary or personal terms. Value is personal, as one person's treasure could be another person's garbage. *Cantville* did not center on the value of money but rather, the value of a person's character and friendship. Everyone should value the important people in their life. Identify your value and give it freely— whether it is money, time or love—they are all equally important. Your value to others builds as you build the value of others. —What do you value? What values do you offer?

Passionate · Prejudgment Resources Productive
Intend Mistake Independent Prejudice Grateful
Routine Free Confidence Content Develop will Excuses
Faith Doubt Define Blame Attitude Assume Accomplish Barrier
Benefit Fear Value
Motivation Impossible Failure
Obstacle Opinion Negative Harmony Positive
Reinforce Trust Responsibility

My Personal Recommended Reading

Animal Farm
By George Orwell

Do it! Let's Get Off Our Buts
By John Roger & Peter McWilliams

Get the Life You Want
By Richard Bandler

Grow Rich!: With Peace of Mind
by Napoleon Hill

If You Had Controlling Parents: How to Make Peace with Your Past and Take Your Place in the World
by Dan Neuharth

I Told My Mind to Shut the F*ck Up... and Then I Saw What Was Possible
by Greg Winick

Jonathan Livingston Seagull
by Richard Bach and Russell Munson

Love Yourself and Let the Other Person Have It Your Way
by Lawrence Crane and Lester Levenson

Shaken: Discovering Your True Identity in the Midst of Life's Storms
by Tim Tebow

Shut up, Stop Whining, and Get a Life: A Kick-Butt Approach to a Better Life
by Larry Winget

The Art of War
by Sun Tzu

The Instant Millionaire
by Mark Fisher

Unlimited Power: The New Science of Personal Achievement
by Tony Robbins

The Way to Love: The Last Meditations of Anthony De Mello
by Anthony De Mello

Wherever I Wind Up: My Quest for Truth, Authenticity and the Perfect Knuckleball.
by Y.A. Dickey with Wayne Coffey

The Wizard's Wish: Or How He Made the Yuckies Go Away-A Story About the Magic in You.
by Brad Yates

About the Author

Joe Borelli is an entrepreneur and successful business owner. In lieu of traditional higher education he opted to attend the,"school of hard knocks." He was self taught through books, and the teachings of self help masters. He credits part of his education from observing and learning from the success and lack of success of others. He believes that his decades of personal trial and error experiences has given him a unique perspective on life. Joe was a serious martial arts practitioner for 15 years, and while no longer active, he still maintains and utilizes the mental aspects of that training. Joe was born and raised in New Jersey, where he resides with his two daughters and trusting beagle. He enjoys family time, the outdoors, the indoors, spending time alone, spending time with friends, comic books, ice cream and everything each new day brings!
Visit him at: www.borellidirectpublishing.com

About the Illustrator

Sergio Drumond is a painter, illustrator, animator and digital graphic artist with various degrees in Fine Arts and Advertising Art. He studied art at Escola de Belas Artes, Bahia, Brazil; painting at Goethe Institut under German painter Adam Firnekaes and engraving with engraver and Bahia Art Museum curator Emanuel Araujo. His portfolio includes illustrating for books and magazines, graphic novels, newspapers and television. He lived in Europe where he worked on book illustrations and magazines as well as posters for theater companies. He spent a great part of his life in the Philippines, Japan, India and Thailand where he worked illustrating books and graphic novels, editing educational videos and doing animation. While in Asia he also taught art for humanitarian projects.
You can contact him at: sdrumondart7@gmail.com